Kippax
in old picture postcards volume 3

including Astley, Allerton Bywater, Brigshaw, Ledston Luck and Gt. Preston

Edgar N. Pickles

European Library ZALTBOMMEL/THE NETHERLANDS

Acknowledgements

The author would like to thank the following people and organizations for the use of their photographs: Allerton Bywater Resource Group, Mr. J. Baldwin, Mr. D. Babbington, Mr. E.J. Brook, Mrs. P. Brook, Mrs. J. Brunt, Mrs. J. Carter, Mrs. R.E. Coates, Miss A. Dunwell, Miss M. Goodall, Friends of the B-E 1150 B Dragline, Mr. B. Fothergill, Mr. A. Harkins, Mrs. J. Holmes, Mr. B. Hope, Prof. G. Howson, Kippax & District Historical Society, Kippax Parish Church Council, Mr. G. Parkinson, Mr. T. Parkinson, Mrs. M. Rhodes, Skyrack Express, Mr. J. Smith, Mr. B. Stringer, Mrs. J. Taylor, Mrs. E. Walker, late Mr. N. Webb, Mrs. S. Williamson W.M.D.C. (Castleford Library).

My thanks to Mr. M.D.L. Brumwell and my wife Beryl for reading the manuscript.

This book is dedicated to my wife Beryl for all her help.

GB ISBN 90 288 3558 x

European Library
post office box 49
NL – 5300 AA Zaltbommel/The Netherlands
telephone: 0031 418 513144
fax: 0031 418 515515
e-mail:publisher@eurobib.nl

Introduction

It was a very pleasant surprise to be asked to do a third volume of pictures of Kippax; I did not think there would be enough photographs of such a fairly small village, which it was until about one hundred years ago. There was indeed nearly sufficient material, so it was decided to make up the shortfall with illustrations of surrounding villages and hamlets, none of which will be likely to produce a large number of pictures. Astley is now a 'lost village' having disappeared completely when the St. Aidan's Opencast Site destroyed it.

Some people may be surprised by the introduction of industrial history in the shape of the picture of R. B. 1150B 'Oddball', which as far as I am aware is the only preserved dragline machine in Europe. Machines like this were responsible for the removal of places like Astley and Kippax Park House, and for reshaping some of the surrounding areas of Kippax.

Opencast mining is the last form of mining in our area, from the early 'Bell Pits' to opencast, mining has almost gone full circle now. Bell pit mining was done by digging down to coal, which was near to the ground surface, through a narrow opening, then spreading out until the roof was in danger of collapsing. The mine was then abandoned and a new one dug close by. The remains of 'Bell Pits' can be found near where R. B.1150B is on view.

Kippax is changing, just like almost every other town and village in the country, and there have been some changes since the last volume was published in 1997. 'Butterfields' shop on Cross Hills has been demolished as it became unsafe, some shops have been converted into houses and more are planned to do the same. There is new development on 'The Intake', changing the appearance of Kippax when seen from Gt. Preston and Brigshaw. Where the old farmhouse site was on the corner of Gibson Lane / High Street there are to be houses/flats.

Gibson Lane School is to be extended, the old school on Leeds Road will then no longer be required, and Brigshaw High School is in the process of being partially rebuilt after the fire in April 2000, which destroyed a large part of it.

All the villages included in this book, with the exception of Ledston Luck, are very old, Ledsham has evidence of the Romans and the church is the oldest standing building in West Yorkshire. Allerton Bywater is recorded in medieval times and Roman coins have been found in the vicinity. Astley is known to have been the site for a coal mine in the eighteenth century. Gt. Preston is another ancient village, which may have derived its name from 'Priestown', linked to Kippax Church, which, it is thought, could have been a minster church: one which trained priests.

There have been a few people who have become well known or famous from Kippax, Alfred Austin, who's family inter married with the family of Thomas Fawcett of Castleford(maltsers), became poet laureate; John Piper, who was a missionary to China; and Ben Picard, who was the first person from Kippax to become an M.P.

Finally many thanks to all the people who have said how much they like the previous volumes, I hope they and everyone else will enjoy this book.

1 Very few people will remember Kippax as it was in this early view of Cross Hills. The old White Swan was rebuilt in 1915 and Bentley's, the brewers of Woodlesford, were taken over by Whitbreads many years ago. The stone building showing the gable end is now a taxi office and all the cottages beyond it up the High Street have been removed.

2 Cross Hills from a similar view point as the previous photograph, when the Midland Bank (now part of HSBC) had a branch here. To its right was an early self service store, the fish and chip shop is still in business. Across the road the empty shop was Gallons, the grocers, and the shops and flats development is awaiting tenants.

3 West end of High Street, a sign of things to come, with an empty shop next to the bank. The Barclay's Bank, to the right of the pedestrian and the Leeds and Holbeck B.S., which was built in the space where the posters are, all became redundant and the building society office is now an estate agent's office.

4 The bakers and confectioners is still trading today but not as D. Taylor. It is worth noting that this is one of the early occasions when frozen foods are seen to be offered for sale.

5 Harcourt's Cash Stores was situated where the present travel agents are now. Pure white flour is offered for sale at 1/2 d. per stone and custard powder is free with a tin of fruit or a 1 lb. of prunes.

6 This appears to be a Sunday School outing, most probably from the Belgrave Chapel seen in the background on the right. On the left is the former lodge to The Hall which eventually became the Kippax Co-operative Society's Butchery department before it was demolished.

7 Free Church Choir (Belgrave Chapel) posing in front of the back entrance to The Hall. Left to right, back row: A.N. Other, Leonard Appleyard, W. Smith, A. Firth, B. Smith, D. Smith, Herbert Halliday, Levi Plows and Joe Ratcliffe. Second row: Wilfred Halliday (organist), Joe Farrant, Bertha Townend, Alice Goodall, Harold Halliday and Jo Dickson. Third row: Alberta Tillotson, Evelyn Firth, Bertha Halliday, Colin Firth (conductor), Blanche Halliday, Lily Appleyard and Elsie Gummerson. Front row: Anne Firth, Janet Snowdon, Kitty Barratt and Hilda Firth.

8 One of the better pictures of The Hall which survives, this shows it at its best. The gardens are well cared for, not divided up, and the building is in good condition.

9 This group represents a way of life which is largely no more, the maid and mistress are easy to see, but what of the third person in the trio?

10 A late evening shot of The Hall taken from Hall Park Croft soon after the latter was built.

11 The bungalow was at one time part of a small holding and there were animals in the garden. This, as all other buildings in this locality, was cleared away to form the entrance to the new estate of Orchard Croft. The dilapidated remains of The Hall can be seen against the sky.

12 Park View and Manor Terrace are still here, but 'The Intake' surrounding them has been developed to form Orchard Croft, a collection of tall yellow and red brick houses as seen from the south.

13 A family group taken outside No. 6 Hanover Square. Allan Harkins, the baby, with his mother Elizabeth Smith, his aunt and cousins.

14 The first of two pictures of one of Kippax's Carnivals, this one took place in 1973 or 1974 and the Parade is passing the end of Westfield Lane. Isobel McDermot was the Queen that year, the men in 'Mountie' style hats were a group of men who called themselves something like 'Legion of Frontiersmen'.

15 The second of the Carnival photographs, the Queen is passing the Co-operative stores preceded by the Kippax Band. Band conductor Norman Morley is immediately behind the Special Sergeant on the left of the picture. The band members are, from left to right, front row: Arthur Taylor, Bill Teal, Geoff. Church and Arthur Rogers. Second row: Harry Wilkinson, Trevor Parsons, Roy Nicholson and David Morley. Drums Reg. Morley. Third row: ?, ?, Jack Smith, Jack Smith sen. and Matty. Bowers. Forth row: Gordon Murray, Irvine Nicholson, Barry Nicholson, Brian Nicholson and Charles Bailey.

16 Band Practice in the Royal Oak, before Kippax Band got its own premises in the 'Band Club' in the early 70's. From left to right, back row: Bill Teal and Geoff. Church. Middle row: Roy Nicholson and Trevor Parsons. Front row: Andy Allen, Jack Smith and Irvine Nicholson. Far right: Leslie Storey.

17 A World War Two photograph of an unknown lady raising the pointer on the Savings mean More Ships board, which was situated near the junction of High Street and Church Lane. The lady on the left in WREN's uniform is Bertha Backhouse.

18 The former Arthur Rhodes butcher's shop looks as if it may have once have been a farmhouse, it has now become a restaurant. During the course of the alterations a central back-to-back pair of fireplaces were revealed and a seventeenth-century style window with stone mullions.

19 New Street can just be seen in the background of this view through 'Jumbo's Nick', which is situated to the right of the shop window in the previous picture. The nickname is derived from a story of a travelling circus trying to make a short cut through this ginnel, which narrows towards the High Street, and the elephant got stuck. How do you reverse an elephant? Enid Walker on the left and her companion Margaret Adams have plenty of space.

20 Fenton Square was located off the High Street on the south side near The Hall and was cleared with it to make way for the new supermarket and shops. The buildings were ancillary to The Hall which they resembled in appearance but on a reduced scale. The gable end seen just behind the street lamp was the Co-operative house.

21 The Pentecostal Hall on Park Avenue when it was still in use as a church, a reduced congregation led to its eventual closure and demolition. The church has been replaced by a detached house.

22 This 1957 building replaced the pre-World War II 'Tin Heaven' which had been used to provide school dinners for schools in the locality. This structure was used by a retired persons organization for many years, as well as others, for meetings. Finally it was demolished about 1995.

23 'Kitty' Parker, who was the local midwife for many years in Kippax, posing with the church tower in the background.

24 A very old faded photograph of Kippax Church from the south east corner of the churchyard, showing the chancel before it was reordered to a steeply pitched roof and the parapet removed. Note the 'spitters' on the chancel and nave parapets to shed the rain water off the church.

25 The interior of Kippax Church as it was at the end of the Victorian era. The church was extensively renovated in this period.

26 A later view of the inside of Kippax Church looking east in 1949. The chandeliers seen in some of the earlier pictures have been removed and the lighting is now by electricity. The communion rails, altar gates, pulpit and all the plaster on the walls have now been removed. The internal stone work has been painted with limewash to allow the walls to breathe.

27 An unusual event in 1950 when the parish church had two Rose Queens in the same year. The annual Rose Queen at that time was elected by the Sunday School children, and on this unique occasion equal votes were cast for two girls: Moira Bradley on the left and Maureen Briggs on the right of the pageboys. The retiring Rose Queen, Clarice Fellows, is at rear centre. Fourth from left back row is the author's wife, then Beryl Sutcliffe. Maiden names have been used for all the girls.

28 Laying the foundation stone for St. Mary's Church Hall on 15 July 1936 is Mrs. N. de Petheny O'Kelly (nee Bland).

29 The Wesleyan Chapel School Room, seen on the left, was built on to the original chapel, which is rendered and has a higher roofline. In the space between the old chapel and the stone wall were the Almshouses. The car dates this picture to about 1976.

30 Adjoining the Wesleyan schoolroom was the caretakers house; this whole complex together with the chapel across the road was demolished and a modern all-purpose chapel/hall was built on this site.

31 Interior view of the Wesleyan Chapel which was built in 1870. This chapel was demolished and the site reused for a row of houses.

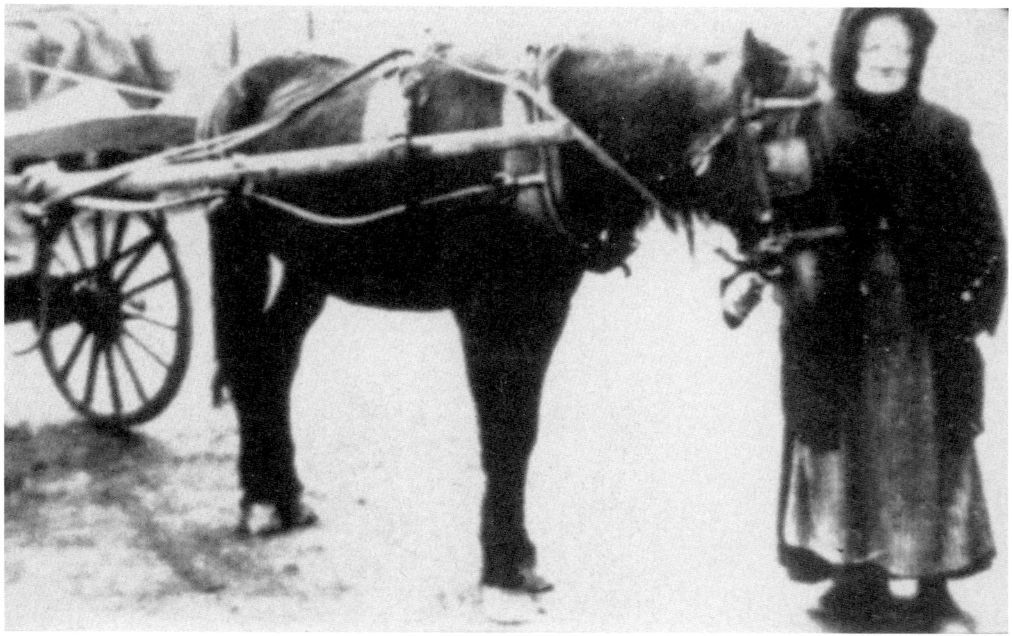

32 This picture of a woman leading a horse and cart is thought to be more than a hundred years old.

33 Not the same horse and cart outside the White Swan Inn on Cross Hills at the back of this group of mainly children. On the left are the Primitive Chapel and the old school where the library is now.

34 The shop on Cross Hills at the top of Well Lane, is best remembered as 'Butterfields' after the last persons to trade there, who traded for many years as greengrocers and wet fishmongers. The premises had originally been a farmhouse, became a shop, later used as a show room for the Gas Board, jointly with the half nearest Well Lane as the Library, and finally returned to retailing.

35 This small scale open-cast operation took place where The Moorgate is now. Sir Lindsay Parkinson's company later became a major construction one.

36 The Moorgate taken on the day it first opened.

37 Moorleigh has expanded since this picture was taken, when it was a private residence. It is now a nursing home.

38 This illustration of a small boy playing in the Sheffield Beck is nicely framed by the arch of the culvert under the railway. The boy is Barry Hope.

39 The new graveyard from 'Tablands', this part of the burial ground is now full, the gable ends of Hopewell and Bargess Terraces and the roof of the Wesleyan Chapel can be seen.

40 Silas Prince here seen using his scythe is where Greenfield School is now. The greenhouses in the background are Lyndum Nurseries.

41 Faith Shackleton used to run The Tuck Shop when the first house called The Hall (see volume 1, p. 73) was a private boys' school. She was said to walk to Garforth railway station in order to travel to Leeds for supplies for the shop, and on her return journey from Garforth carried a basket on each arm and one on her head.

42 A very rustic appearance to what is now the area populated by Oxford Drive and Cambridge Grove.

43 Mary Pannel Hill, although this card, which was posted in 1904, says Castleford, the road is the boundary between Kippax and Ledston. The hill is named after Mary Pannel, who was executed for witchcraft in 1603.

44 Mr. R. Coates, who was a well-known conjuror in his time.

45 This occasion is thought to be a double wedding in Kippax.

46 Kippax Park was built with a south facing aspect, in a deer park. The village of Kippax is to the left and The Home Farm (all which remains of the contemporary buildings) on the right. In the foreground are the offices of the former N.C.B., now awaiting a new use on the edge of what will become a large extension to the village of Allerton Bywater. The park was opencasted in the late 1950's to 1960's destroying the remains of the house, which was derelict by the time this picture was taken.

47 It is thought that the man in this snapshot is the chauffeur to John Davison Bland of Kippax Park, and the two women may be part of the staff there. Kippax Park was abandoned after the sale of the contents in 1929.

48 Kippax Park was the most splendid house ever erected in Kippax. This was the main entrance on the south front. Sir John Bland refaced the original Elizabethan house of three bays, extended the house and added long wings. This view gives some idea of the grandeur of the house, even as it was decaying.

49 The east wing of Kippax Park appears almost complete here but a look at the main part of the house shows the roof timbers exposed. This and the previous photograph were taken just before the house was demolished.

50 The ornate nature of the interior of Kippax Park can be seen in the detail of one of the fireplaces. It is not known where in the house this was, but it appears from the sale catalogue that only the removable items were sold, not fixtures.

51 All the tables, chairs, pictures, etc. were sold when the contents of Kippax Park were auctioned in October 1929. This room is identified as The Green Room, from the sale catalogue. The black tables are early Georgian, painted over the gilding.

52 Kippax Station when it was well known for its prize winning floral displays.

53 An early look at Kippax Station, from the top of the embankment opposite the station, before the signal box was added to the right-hand end of the station building. In the background can be seen the Station Cottages. This picture is reproduced from a glass slide suitable for projection by a 'Magic Lantern'.

54 This bus driver and his conductor posing here on the top of Leeds Road probably worked for Kippax and District Motor Co. The gable end of part of the Leeds Road School can be seen over the wall behind the bus.

55 Woodend in the days when mining was carried on the conventional way at Bowers Row; this coal train is been hauled from the marshalling yard connected to Victoria and Albert Pits by an ex. War Department locomotive. The Fish and Chip Shop is hidden by the bus and the Edward VII Club is off the picture to the right. Note the crossing man's cabin.

56 The line from Bowers Row joined the 'main' line at Bowers Halt. This Q6 Class locomotive is waiting for the signal to clear so it can join its train, possibly to bring it up from Bowers. Almost all traces of the railway have been removed now and the former route is a public footpath.

57 A group of platelayers seen with their trolley at Bowers Halt about 1950. They are, left to right, Gordon Harding (ganger), 'Jocky' Hargreaves, Dennis Prince and Arthur Stephenson. The line to Bowers curves off to the left behind them.

58 The Angel Inn has been demolished very recently and is to be replaced by a nursing home. The Angel is mentioned in Trade Directories, and it was at one time well known in the district for the concert parties held there.

59 Where this shop once stood in Allerton Bywater at the junction of Main Street and Leeds Road are now a small garden and the bus stop.

60 The Manor House in Allerton Bywater was demolished to allow housing development to take place on the eastern side of Main Street about 1988. There was a Manor of Allerton Bywater from at least medieval times, but it is difficult to put a date on this house from these pictures. The gable end was of brick, as was the lean-to section. The left-hand side was double storeyed and the other one appeared to be single, giving an uneven roof line.

61 The other part of the 'L'-shaped Manor House was of stone construction, which may indicate it was the older part. The sash windows may not have been the original ones, there is evidence of brickwork above the lower window, which sometimes means that some masonry collapsed at some time, may be when 'new' windows were put in.

62 The chimney shown in this picture of Allerton Bywater Colliery was later removed when the winding gears were electrified. The two headgear's and engine houses are clearly visible.

63 Ledston Station and Allerton Bywater Colliery are both lost to us now. Ledston Station was almost identical to the one at Kippax, and on the same line of The Leeds, Castleford, and Pontefract Junction Railway Company, to give the branch its full title, when it was formed in 1873.

64 This superb view of Allerton Bywater Colliery between 1919 and 1939, when it was in private ownership as part of Airedale Collieries. The shafts are to the right and the coalwasher is to the centre left.

65 Coal from Allerton Bywater Colliery was transported by barge on The Aire and Calder Navigation as well as by rail. Large volumes of coal could be moved by water, and still are. This picture of coal loading taking place at the staithes near The Boat Inn in the 1950's was a common sight at the time.

66 Kippax from Brigshaw, the houses on the left are still there but all the tree covered areas in the foreground are built on now.

67 An aerial view of Brigshaw Farm, the farm was on Brigshaw Lane near the entrance to the present Brigshaw High School, which was pulled down because mining subsidence had made it uninhabitable. Mr. E. Fothergill farmed there until 1968.

68 'Oddball' was so named because of its unusual combination of electrical components. It is one of the few preserved draglines in the world. Officially called a B. E. 1150B, it was manufactured in the USA in 1948 and worked there for four years until it came to Britain to work in South Wales. The machine was then moved to the Midlands and finally to St. Aidan's site, where it worked until the 'great flood', when the River Aire broke its north bank and flooded the opencast mine workings. After the mine was drained it was decided to scrap 'Oddball', and a preservation group was formed to save it.

69 The village of Astley, was 'lost' when the St. Aidan's Opencast Site removed it in the 1970's. The road from Bowers Row to Swillington was realigned to allow this. It is not known how old the hamlet was, but it is shown on old maps of the area. This view is looking east and shows the Old Farm House.

70 Stanley House in Astley has a very rural aspect, even though it was only a short distance from Bowers Row and was served by a regular bus service.

71 The signpost gives us a clue to where this is in Gt. Preston – most of the houses are still there today – where Berry Lane meets Preston Lane / Whitehouse Lane.

72 The Old Hall, Gt. Preston, was for many years used as The Workhouse of this area. When it was pulled down some of the Jacobean panelling was re-used in St. Aidan's Church to panel the Sanctuary.

73 St. Aidan's Church on Preston Lane was always part of the Parish of Kippax. The church was a red-brick one, built on land donated by the Lowther family of Swillington. For many years the Curate of the parish lived in the village, but in later years the curate's house was sold and a house purchased in Kippax for that purpose. The Church School is to the right of the church.

74 Ledston Luck was so named when Lady Wheler, here shown digging the first sod for the new shaft of Ledston Luck Colliery, was quoted as saying 'Let us have luck in this place'. The colliery was started in 1909, closed for a period in the 1930's and finally closed in 1987.

75 Ledston Luck Colliery almost at the end of its life. The old style telephone box and bus shelter have both been replaced now.

76 The Orphanage in Ledsham, founded by Lady Elizabeth Hastings in the eighteenth century, closed many years ago, but this scene reminds us of times when the state did not take care of everything.